SECOND CHANCES

by Mary Williams

Edited by Meg Wegs

Cover artwork by author

With great reluctance, great humbleness, and great thankfulness, I have opened the door to a very dark closet and let the light shine in!!!

Printed by CreateSpace, An Amazon.com Company

Edited by Meg Wegs

❧ *Preface* ❧

In this wonderful, free country we think of orphanages as existing in the third world or formerly Communist nations.

But the dark truth is that they have existed in this country. They are called by other names. I lived in an orphanage from a young age until I was sixteen years old.

The years passed. At the age of sixty I became a Baha'i. It was without hesitation even though I was happy in my religion and was not looking for a change. This became the beginning of a whole new life. I have never looked back to what I loved and practiced for sixty years.

❧ *Contents* ❧

❧ Second Chances ❧

Do you always have a second chance? **Always**

Who are given second chances? **Everyone**

Do you get a second chance no matter what you have done? **Yes**

Are you responsible for the chances you took and the results? **Perhaps**

Are you responsible if you took a chance without having the knowledge you NEEDED before taking the chance? **No**

Do second chances always work? **Absolutely not**

Are young children responsible for taking chances? **Not always**

Chapter 1 ~ *I was the Duty*

I was born at a hospital in Virginia. For some reason I do not know, my mother left me at the hospital when she went home.

That was not a good start in life. After several days an aunt was sent to get me. She kept me for a long time.

My mother was from a large family; many families were large in those days. I was passed around from aunt to uncle; each relative kept me for a long time.

I don't remember who, but someone took me to Sunday School. I was probably around four years old. I learned little songs, stories, but most important, I learned about God and how to pray. I learned that God could hear and would answer our prayers.

During those years I learned to adjust to the routine of each family. I was not a family member. I was considered a family duty. I had to obey and stay in the background as much as possible. I never knew love and acceptance in those years.

Chapter 2 ~ *Waiting for my Mother*

As soon as I was old enough to be accepted, I was taken to an orphanage on a mountaintop. It was so beautiful there. I could look down in the valley and see for miles and miles.

On rare occasions my mother came to see me. She would write and let me know the date she would come. It was always on a Sunday.

I would sit in the grass from early morning and watch the roads in the valley. I waited to see the car coming up the road leading to the orphanage. It was just a dot in the distance, but I knew it was her. My mother was coming to see me.

When I first received her letter, I started praying that she was coming to take me home. She never did of course. When she left I went back to my place in the grass and still hoped she would come and get me. I prayed with all my heart that the car would turn around and come back for me. She would surprise me. I would wait until I knew enough time had passed that I knew for sure she would not be taking me home,

I loved her so much. I thought she was the most perfect person in the world. Each time I would ask myself, "Why doesn't she come back for me?". Next time I needed to pray harder and then she would take me home.

Chapter 3 ~ *Work and Awful Soap*

By the time I was eleven years old, another girl and I would awake at four A.M. We had to walk in the dark to the dining hall. In the kitchen we prepared breakfast for two hundred and fifty people. An adult dietician developed the menu we used. Ovens were huge; some were used to keep the food warm. The other two meals were prepared by a professional staff which came from town. We always had milk at every meal. The orphanage had a herd of cattle, and the cows were allowed to roam in the fields where onions were growing. The milk would taste like green onions. The children did not drink that milk unless they were told to taste it….there was nothing to be done about that milk. When each meal was over, all the tablecloths had to come off, and clean ones spread. All the chairs were moved, the floor swept and scrubbed. Chairs were put back and the tables were set for the next meal.

About the soap! One of my clearest memories is of the soap we used in our personal needs. It was a large, green bar. It had a terrible odor! It was so big I couldn't get my small hands around it. This was used to wash my hair and to take a shower. I washed my clothes with that soap on a metal scrubbing board. Older girls were assigned to help the younger girls. The all-purpose soap! Everyone was treated equally — all ages.

Cleaning teeth? We had powdered tooth cleaner that came in a box. I sprinkled some in my hand and used my fingers to rub it over my teeth. Then I cupped my hands together and rinsed my mouth. Cups were not available.

I soon learned to mind my house mother, and to walk away from any argument. Anyone who was arguing would get the same punishment from the "cat of nine tails". It was a dowel about two feet long with nine strips of rawhide nailed to the end. I learned to keep quiet and not to argue. After two painful beatings I chose the shelter of silence. A hesitancy to speak was the result. This stayed a part of my personality for much of my life causing problems difficult to overcome.

The housemothers lived on the grounds permanently; they did not have training for the position. Discipline was done in different ways depending on who the housemother was. I had the same housemother all the years I was there. I knew what the rules were.

There was never a lack of playmates since twenty-five girls lived in my dormitory. At first I was quiet and shy; in free time we played together. We didn't have toys so we had to use our imagination. We built forts and playhouses outside with branches. We ran and played in a large attic on rainy days. We really had fun in any free time we had.

Chapter 4 ~ *Old Clothes and New Clothes*

Twice a year we were given a complete set of new clothes. The times were Easter and when school started in August. Two pairs of socks a year didn't last – we did so much walking they soon had holes in the heels. We sewed holes up so many times we finally had to wear them with the holes in them. We walked one mile to Church and a mile back; and walked two miles to school and two miles to return.

I was eleven years old just before Easter. I was frying eggs for breakfast when the grease in the pan caught on fire. It burned my arms, hands, and everywhere my upper body was exposed. A few days later was Easter Sunday and I couldn't wear my new clothes. I didn't think ABOUT THE BURNS. I was all bandaged and the NEW DRESS WOULD NOT FIT OVER ALL THAT! I wore an old dress and looked on as the other girls looked so pretty in their new clothes.

Chapter 5 ~ *Early School Days*

My small world was the buildings for the girls; the boys had other buildings. The dining hall and Chapel were located between the buildings. In the dining hall the girls were on one side and the boys on the opposite side. The girls were not allowed to talk to a boy and the boys could not talk to a girl. SOMETIMES A GIRL SAW A BOY IN THE HALL THAT SHE THOUGHT SHE WOULD LIKE, BUT IT NEVER WENT BEYOND A WISH. In the buildings where we lived, we did not have television or radio and no telephones. We didn't know what these were. There were no newspapers so there was no way to know what was happening beyond the walls. When I went to school I came in contact with other children, but they tended to stay away from the children of the orphanage.

I started school, and liked the classes. I worked hard to learn to read and print and later to write. My favorite subject was reading. I sounded out the syllables. Soon I could read all the books in the first grade, I had one big problem. I was left-handed but that was not permitted. Teachers forced me to learn to write with my right hand. My mind was very confused about this and I became dyslexic. I still get my right and left hand confused.

I was allowed to skip second grade and went to third grade. I believe this was because I could read so well. I don't have any way to know for sure.

As I grew older, I read everything I could get my hands on. At night when the lights were turned off, I had a flashlight and I would pull the covers over my head, no one could see light under the covers. With the flashlight on I read until late in the night. I don't know where the flashlight and batteries came from; I just remember having them.

Chapter 6 ~ *Meeting Black People on My Shortcut*

After I had finished working in the dining hall or kitchen, I had to return to the dormitory, change to my school dress, get my books, and walk to school. If I walked the regular route, I would be late, but that was not acceptable by the school staff.

I found a short cut on a road between some small houses with fenced in yards. No one knew I was walking on this short cut. From their windows some people noticed me walking while carrying books. I had never seen people like this before, and I was uneasy. After a few weeks some people came outside, smiled and waved at me. I smiled and waved back. I had no reason not to wave back even though their skin color was different than mine.

As time passed some men, women, and children began walking with me until the road ended. Then I could walk by the street that led to the school. We were talking by then and I said goodbye to them. I felt protected when they walked with me. I wasn't alone on the road anymore. When I used the shortcut, I was never late.

Chapter 7 ~ *A New Friend*

Since I was a loner and so shy, I spent time each day reading my Bible and praying. I don't know if you would say I was spiritually inclined. I didn't know what those words meant. We had to attend services in the Chapel on Sunday afternoon and also Wednesday evening.

The time came when I heard the missionaries in CHINA had to leave the country. The Communists were killing all the missionaries they could find.

Ms. Elizabeth Reynolds had been in CHINA ALL HER ADULT LIFE. She did not want to leave. The Church that was sponsoring her told her that for the safety of her life she had to return to the States.

Ms. Reynolds came to work at the orphanage where I lived.She was given an apartment in the main building. I don't know what her position was called. I just know what she came to mean to me.

Ms. Reynolds taught all the very young children about Jesus and God. They were called "Sunbeams". They learned simple songs and Bible stories. She explained the meaning of some short Bible verses. I worked with her to keep the children in order.

Soon I sang the little songs with them and even told them simple Bible stories. Best of all they learned to say A PRAYER AT MEAL TIME AND OTHER SHORT PRAYERS. Helping the children meant I could have more time with Ms. Reynolds in her office.

When the other girls were talking and visiting between chores, I would spend that time with Ms. Reynolds. She was so kind and soft spoken. I had never met anyone like her before.

We went to Church on Sunday morning in the town. We were not allowed to miss. It was my choice to belong to the choirs and to walk back to the night service. It was always dark as I walked home at night, usually alone, but I WAS NEVER AFRAID. I don't remember any crime to worry about at that time, but I wouldn't have heard about it anyway.

There was a program at Church called the "Forward Steps". Ms. Reynolds taught the girls who wanted to participate. The program had requirements for each step. We had to memorize Bible verses. The passages became longer as we climbed the steps. Sitting in Ms. Reynolds office, I studied and memorized the passages required of me. We had to do many other activities, which were centered on the verses of the step we were on.

Every year there was a ceremony in which each person in "Forward Steps" was recognized for their progress. We wore pretty dresses, and the older girls were on the top steps. It took years to complete the program. I was determined to go all the way to the top.

Ms. Reynolds invited me several times to her apartment. For me it was a different world. Souvenirs from her world travels were displayed. She took time to tell me where each one had come from.

As I marveled in her apartment, I was full of unspoken questions. I thought I wanted to be a missionary when I was old enough. I didn't know just anyone could be one.

Chapter 8 ~ *Flashes of Memory*

This happened when I was ten or eleven years old. It might as well have been yesterday. I never knew how to put anything like this into words, so I didn't. I just lived with it until now. Who would I tell anyway, then or now? Until that night when I walked home after dark, I was never afraid. When I reached the campus, I knew the night watchman was nearby and I was home. That may be why such a horror was so incomprehensible. There were subjects that were not allowed to be known at that time at our home. Necessary things were told in the fewest words possible, leaving us to really not understand any more than after the "short talk". I never related what happened that night to sex. That confusing night would leave me forever with feelings of guilt and helplessness, would I ever feel safe again?

At the orphanage if you had not been disciplined recently, done your chores well, and made good grades the last six weeks, the one treat allowed was to go to a movie on Monday night. On this particular Monday I walked the mile into town with a girl from my building; she was several years older than I. What the movie was, I do not remember .

The lower doorway led to the laundry room and sewing room. There were no doors, only the openings; then up steps that led to the first floor, then up more steps to the dormitory where all the girls were sleeping. JUST AS WE ROUNDED THE CORNER TO GO UP THE STEPS TO THE FIRST FLOOR, A MAN WAS WAITING IN THE SHADOWS. The night watchman was waiting for us. Neither of us saw him. Only flashes of my memory remain for me.

He reached out of nowhere and grabbed both of us from the steps and dragged both of us into the laundry room.

We kicked and screamed and tried to get away. We knew there was no one to hear us. He was stronger than both of us. He began to take my friend's coat off while still holding onto me. He was so busy tearing her clothes off, that he did not notice me as I unbuttoned my coat, slipped my arms out and ran up the steps. Then it was even more difficult for me.

I was so young with little knowledge of life. I was bound by rules and regulations and afraid of punishment. The rule was that when you returned from the movie, we were to knock on the door, and tell the house parent we were back. But both of us were not back, so I did not knock. I slipped fully clothed into my bed, terrified. I had not knocked on the door, and where was my friend? I began praying. I am not sure what I prayed for. I just knew I had to talk to God. "God, please tell me what to do," I begged. Maybe if everything was quiet, he wouldn't come up the steps and get the other girls. If I told the housemother, what would she do? There was no way to contact someone for help. We had no phone. She had no more protection than I did. If he came up the steps he could get more girls and she couldn't stop him. I couldn't think what to do. If I got anyone involved, I didn't know if what happened to my friend might happen to her. I was shaking in my bed, praying to God to help me out of this nightmare. I lay in total dark waiting for the sound of footsteps, so I would know she had broken free. But her steps never came. I heard nothing.

The long, dark night passed and morning came. I did

not have to cook breakfast that morning. There was no mention of my friend. Her sister was asked to stay behind when we left to walk to the dining hall. When we returned the sister was gone and nothing was mentioned about either girl. Surely they knew I had been with my friend. My coat was in the laundry room. No one talked to me or questioned me. It was as if we had never been gone. I was never told what happened. I always had trouble coping with the incident and the silence.

I know now that the night watchman assaulted and murdered my friend. Could I have helped her? How? Was I able to get away because she was older and he started with her first? If only someone had talked to me and helped me understand. Things went on as if life was normal, but it was anything but normal for me. Since I couldn't allow anyone to really know my feelings, my mind repressed them.

I would have episodes where I would go outside my body and know everything that was happening around me. I heard what people were saying. My teacher at school would often ask me a question, but I could not respond. These were my reactions to the shock, terror and deafening silence in the face of the trauma I had experienced. I understand that now. For many years the episodes continued making me feel further removed from everything than I already was. But one thing changed forever. I never have worn a coat the rest of my life; in winter I wear a heavy sweater.

Chapter 9 ~ *My Lost Summer*

As you will soon understand, I have little information about this time. It was at the end of a school year, and I looked forward to wearing shorts and a top and no shoes. I do not remember the day this happened. I only recall it was the end of summer. One day I woke up in the infirmary. It was probably in the afternoon. I wondered why I was there. I did not remember being sick. I looked around and found my clothes. I knew the nurse took a nap in the afternoon. She was too heavy to climb the stairs, and all the infirmary beds were upstairs. I waited until all was quiet for a while. I put on my clothes and quietly walked down the stairs. I opened the door and slipped outside. I walked over the campus to my building. Everyone appeared surprised to see me.

Inside my building I looked at the list of those who were going swimming in half an hour. Only a few from each building could go swimming at one time. There was one opening for this time. I asked my house parent if I could go. She was also surprised to see me. If the nurse had given permission I could go. Quickly I changed clothes and put on my bathing suit. Soon I was in line with the other girls. I looked around, and thought: Oh my goodness, here comes the nurse with a big switch in her hand. I didn't know she could move that fast. I got a good switching all the way back to the infirmary. I had to stay two more weeks. When I came back it was time to start back to school. I have always called this "my lost summer" because I didn't know where it went.

Chapter 10 ~ *Questions for My Future*

MY TEENAGE YEARS DID NOT MAKE LIFE EASIER FOR ME. I wasn't comfortable with who I was or where I was, or where I was going. I had already decided what I wanted to do with my life. I took the school subjects that would allow me to be accepted in a college. I had no experience in everyday life outside the orphanage but surely someone would prepare me for that. Society assumed that everyone knew how to find a store and buy a loaf of bread, or how to find and use a pay phone. I knew nothing about the worth of merchandise. How much did a pair of socks cost? I had never held an entire dollar in my hand before. The world was beyond my reach. The out-of-body experiences became worse after school started.

I FELT LIKE TWO PERSONS: one, the shy, quiet girl they saw; the other, a confused girl with too many memories tucked away deep inside. I simply built a wall around myself, for protection.

Beginning eighth grade meant starting high school. The building was three stories high, with a set of stairs on each end. For the first time I had a different teacher for each subject. This was most distressing to me. With my confusion of left and right, the out-of-body experiences, and everyday stress, navigating to classes each day became a horror. It depended which door I came out of as to which staircase I needed to use. Each subject was in a different room. Even though I was at that school for five years and five days a week, the new schedule made getting to class like a maze for me.

Finally I figured out a plan that might work for me. I would come out of my class, look in the hallway for someone I knew would be in my next class and follow her. It meant I had to carry all my books; I couldn't go to my locker. I couldn't take a bath room break, or I would lose sight of that person. Many times I missed lunch because my "guide" had a different lunchtime. I had to wait and watch for my "guide". If that person was absent, I was just lost. When I missed a class, I needed a written excuse the next day, which of course I didn't have. I would be sent to the principal's office which I could not find. How could no one notice the difficulties I was having? I barely knew when the teacher asked me a question. How could the school teachers and counselors not notice I had problems?

Chapter 11 ~ *Chores and Homework*

Chores and homework had to be done after school. We took turns cleaning the dining room after dinner, and after breakfast in the morning.

After dinner everyone met downstairs to do homework. A person could not leave until the homework was completed, or a certain amount of time had passed. There was never an excuse for not doing the homework. One was punished if the homework was not ready for the next day.

After the study time if you were lucky, you could take a

quick bath before bedtime. We had just one shower and one tub, for the twenty-five of us girls. When I had my turn, I used the horrible green soap for showering, and washing my hair. We also learned to wash a few clothes in the water, wring them and take and hang them on our steel bed to dry. Some of the older girls were assigned to help young children with bathing and washing some clothes.

On Saturdays we did the weekly cleaning of all the living areas. Doing all that work was exhausting. I think all of us were happy that the next day was Sunday when we were expected to attend Church services.

I still had my friend, Ms. Reynolds. I spent as much time with her as I could. How else could I have lived there? She did not know about my private problems. I always had the unanswered question: Why didn't my mother take me home?

Chapter 12 ~ *Better Days in School*

Most of my learning in school was through reading. I also used the library as a great resource. I had a difficult time with math in the eighth grade, but made it up in the ninth grade. I needed the credit so I could take trigonometry for I wanted an academic diploma. That year and the next I took many of my favorite classes: Latin, Greek Mythology, History, English Grammar and English Literature.

I loved literature, and wrote several short plays; the teacher produced them and the students in the class played the parts. I wrote poetry which I still enjoy writing. The other solace I had during this time was singing in the choir. As the orphanage was supported by several churches, the churches would request that the choir come and sing at their service. We would travel to a church, and stay with families of Church members, returning back the next day.

Chapter 13 ~ *God and Me*

The experiences of my youth were difficult with stresses and challenges, beyond what most girls have. Yet as a constant presence in my life from an early age, for which I was most grateful, was my relationship with God. Through His good graces I have been able to withstand hardship and still accomplish much. Many nights I would not be able to sleep, but praying always gave me a little peace.

When I was young, I did not understand many events that are clear to me now. In those early years, I often went to sit on the grass looking down on the valley below and prayed, by myself. It was my one special place. Maybe that helped me so I did not give up.

When I was older, I prayed that I would make it through each day without getting lost or embarrassing myself in front of others.

The events in the ensuing years after school would test anyone's Faith, but through it all I could feel God by my side.

Chapter 14 ~ *A Promise to Keep*

As we became older the housemother would assign some of us to be responsible for the younger children on Sunday. Duties: to make sure they were clean and dressed and get them to Sunday school on time; it also included making sure they sat still, did not talk during the sermon, and not be distracting. We leaders would be severely reprimanded if any girl in one's care misbehaved. I took the job seriously.

One Sunday a little girl was assigned to me. I wanted to impress my housemother with how good I could get her to behave. I promised her something special if she would be good during Church. There was a house on the corner that we walked past on our way. An apple tree was in the back yard. I promised the child that if she was good , I'd give her an apple.

I was sure she would forget about it. As we approached the house, she said, "Don't forget you will get an apple for me if I was good!" There was nothing for me to do but keep my word. In my Sunday dress, hose and high heels, I shimmied up the tree in the stranger's yard.

Just then the Director of the orphanage came riding by in a car and saw me in the tree. The car stopped and he came out the door. He told me in no uncertain terms to come to his office as soon as I was back. I was terrified! In all my years there, I had never been to the Director's office. I knew it meant nothing good was in store for me. On the way home the young child was happy as a lark eating her apple, while I was filled with dread thinking of the meeting in the office.

Once we were back, I told the child to change her dress, and I made my way to the office. The Director was a heavy man. He gave me no time for an explanation. He pulled his belt from around his waist, and gave me a good whacking. It was the first and last time I would see that office. I learned a lesson that Sunday, but not from a preacher.

The little girl was happy with her apple; the housemother was relieved that all went well in Church. I was the only person unhappy at how things turned out.

Chapter 15 ~ *Dating Time*

When we became of dating age, certain rituals were met before any boy could call on any of the young women of the orphanage. Only two nights were allowed for dating: Friday or Saturday. We could go on only one night. The boy had to come to the cottage and meet with the housemother. She decided whether or not the boy was suitable. She let them leave or made the young couple stay there and talk in the living room and become more acquainted under her watchful eye.

If the housemother had any qualms about the responsibility of a young man, she would talk to him before bringing down his date from upstairs. The young men who were acceptable had to come inside to pick up his date. The housemother would call the young woman to come downstairs. When dropping off his date, the young man had to bring her inside before leaving. Dates started at seven P.M. and ended at ten P.M.

I dated several boys. My first date was David. I liked him a lot; he took me to meet his mother. But he moved away. He always treated me like a lady and we had dated for a year. We promised to keep in touch but that slowed down after some time.

For some reason another young man noticed me. He was known by name by all the teachers, mainly because he had attempted to pass the eighth grade twice before. He never had his homework, and came and went as he pleased. He stood out in my mind because he was always well-dressed. He wore white buck shoes and his clothes were perfectly matched, often in pink and black, the colors worn by Elvis Presley who was just beginning to get popular. His name was Frank. He persisted in asking me out even though I usually refused. I really didn't want to be alone with him.

I agreed to see a movie with him if he would meet me at the theatre and I wouldn't have to ride with him. I made sure we sat with other girls I knew. I was still young and didn't want to get close with this boy. He did not like seeing me with any other boy.

He would wait for me after school and want to walk me home but I would let him go only part of the way. Besides all the other children were walking all around us. I couldn't decide if I liked him or if I didn't like him. I wasn't sure either way.

It became apparent that he thought of me as his girl. He began waiting for me after CHURCH AND AT FOOTBALL GAMES. Most times I attended games with a group of girls. Invariably, he would sit a few places away. He did not pass eighth grade again, and did not return to school. Education was not important to him, but it was important to me. That year with such a full schedule at school, I didn't go on many dates.

This boy lived on a farm and helped his parents some. Then during the year he was involved in a very bad car accident. He was semi-conscious for about five weeks. His parents told the doctor about me and the doctor suggested that I visit him. Perhaps hearing my voice would wake him. One day he motioned me closer to his bed. When I approached he repeatedly reached for my dress, and tried to rip the buttons off. I didn't return to the hospital again.

Once Frank recovered, he bought a car, and I would see him parked on the street where I had to walk to get home. He had sustained some injuries to his legs, but he could still drive. Later, the use of his legs returned. Frank would try to entice me to let him take me home from school. It was a two mile walk, and I would be walking with other girls. When I refused to ride with him, the other girls were only too happy to pile into his car to ride home. That meant I walked home alone, but I didn't care.

Chapter 16 ~ *My Life Changes Unexpectedly*

I look back at that situation now as similar to every other aspect of my early life. Forces were working together to make me do something I didn't want to do. I was soon to learn this in a life-changing way. I don't know how to tell how things happened. I do not remember every detail.

One day Frank's mother called and talked to my housemother. His mother wanted me to be dressed in Sunday clothes the coming Sunday. They would take me to Church with them and they wanted me to spend the day with them.

When I WAS IN FRANK'S CAR and we had started down the road, I said, "This is not the way to your home." He said his sister had phoned a South Carolina magistrate, and gave his name and my name as new residents of that state for three days. He told me we would be married by a Justice of the Peace. He told me to give my age as 23 when we signed the certificate. The Justice's wife was the witness.

All I could think of was that my dream of college and becoming a nurse were gone. Frank drove us back and I suppose the time was right. I don't remember any complaints. In a few weeks I was so sick every day the nurse thought I had caught the flu. Frank heard about my illness and was pleased his plan was working. His sister made an appointment with a doctor. I would have a baby. I had no idea how this happened. I had not done anything knowingly to cause this.

I was terrified! I wrote to my mother what had happened. What was I to do about having a baby? As soon as my mother received the letter, she came to see me. Mother said, " You have ten minutes to decide. I can't stay longer than ten minutes. You can stay married and keep the baby, or I will take you with me and place you in a home for unwed mothers."

I would have to agree to sign a paper that I would never see the baby again or know anything about its life. Or she could have the marriage annulled because I was only sixteen when he took me over the state line to be married.

How could I make a decision in ten minutes? I had no idea what this would mean to my life. I felt I could never give up my baby whatever it would cost me. I would finally have something that belonged to me. No one could take it away from me. I would give it all my love, and it would love me back. Thinking of this alone I chose to stay married. My mother left after hearing my decision.

Chapter 17 ~ *One Year and No Longer*

I had to pack my things and leave the only place I had

called home that same day. It didn't take long. All that I owned fit into a paper grocery bag. Frank came for me.

We went to his parent's home. They were so happy, and Frank's plan was complete to be married and to have a child. I wanted to run away, but where would I go? Because Frank's father drove a school bus in addition to working his large farm, I was able to attend school. Education was still important to me. No one in his family thought it was important. They had me doing many chores.

While I was in school those last months, I didn't gain weight. I thought no one could notice I was pregnant. But the girls soon knew, and the news spread quickly. My reputation was ruined and they stayed away from me. I still finished the school year.

Now I had to work hard until I was eight months pregnant. I was asked to cook, and clean newly killed chickens, and prepare pig meat to be cut into what each part was used for. I learned how to make sausage. I helped milk cows, churn cream by hand, make cottage cheese, buttermilk, and real butter.

Frank and I lived with his parents for one year. I said, "One year living here and no longer." I had my seventeenth birthday a few months before my baby was born.

Chapter 18 ~ *My First Baby*

As soon as the nurse put my baby in my arms, the first

time, I fell in love. This wasn't like anything I had known before. Loving my baby made my life and work easier. I named him Wayne.

I quickly learned to heat water to give my baby a bath, prepare his bottles with formula, and wash his clothes. He was born in October. When winter came, it was so cold in the mountains and we did not have heat. It was a real problem figuring out how to keep him warm. At night he slept in his bassinet by my bed. He was dressed in warm clothes; a snowsuit over his clothes and wrapped in several blankets, with mittens on his hands. I took a frozen bottle of formula with me when I went to bed. When I heard the baby begin to stir, I put the bottle on the heating pad that was over him. By the time he was really awake I got up and fed him. I uncovered him in one place at a time, and changed his clothes. I covered him up so he was warm again. I went back to bed and we both slept till morning. During the day he lay in a straw clothes basket by a one room heater. He had to be covered carefully always. I had to wash his clothes every day. As I hung the clothing outside, they would freeze which made using clothespins difficult. I always had a long line of cloth diapers, too. I started Wayne in baby class at Church when he was six weeks old.

We had no money and my husband's family felt he should not have to get a job. I had to feed the baby so I lied and said I was eighteen and found a job which was full-time.

I had to pay my mother-in-law to care for Wayne during

the day. I also paid someone to drive me to work and bring me home. At a grocery store I bought baby food for the week.

For work I had just one outfit, so I had to wash it every night. Sometimes I would be so tired, I just could not heat water to wash my outfit, so I wore it the next day anyway. All the girls at work were older and had nice clothes, and could buy lunch at noon. I was ashamed that I worked so hard and still had none of this. It didn't help that I was expected to put gas in the car so my husband could gamble day and night.

I still had the same chores to do when I came home from work. I spent all the time I could with my son, so I didn't mind so much not moving yet.

Chapter 19 ~ *A Strange Marriage*

I had made some friends at work, but I could never invite them to Frank's parent's home. My home was not where I lived.

I began to know I had no real marriage. I had not known how a marriage was supposed to be. As I listened to the ladies at work, I knew that my marriage wasn't like any of theirs. I did not like my marriage. I didn't know what marriage really was. Nobody had ever explained it to me. Perhaps I would have run away if I had known. Even though I had found myself into something I did not want, I was not a quitter. I decided I would do my best to make it work.

Before my son was four months old, I found myself pregnant again. It is hard to believe I still did not know what was causing this. My first daughter, Doris, was born the next November. Again Frank and his family were elated and I was not. I really pushed hard for our place to live now. I told the family if we did not move in a few months, I would take my children and leave.

Frank knew I was serious, so he found a job, and bought a new house-trailer. He had it parked in a trailer park where people lived until they passed away or moved out of town.

When I went to the doctor for a checkup, he asked me, "Do you know what is causing you to be pregnant?"

I had to say, "No, I didn't". The doctor took a long time with me and explained things I should have known before.

There is no need to say we had no babies for seven years. Then it was my choice.

My husband continued to work. We did nothing together. It was a strange marriage. I spent all my time at home. Frank even went to the grocery store for groceries.

Chapter 20 ~ *Is God Listening?*

I had talks with my minister, and as always I prayed for strength to get through the days of physical and mental abuse. I finally felt that God didn't want to hear me anymore. However I prayed and studied my Bible. Surely, there was an answer for me there. My minister's advice was to be strong and righteous and my life would be better. I was told I had to be a better person; that would cause my husband to change. I didn't know how to be better; what could I change?

When Frank found a job running a service station, it brought an unwelcome change. There was a large lot behind the Station with a ten foot slotted fence surrounding it. He had the trailer moved to that lot because he said it would be cheaper. We were cut off from other people. No one would know that we lived there; we could not see out because of the fence.

Sometimes "Grandpa", Frank's father, would come and take my son with him to the stockyard where farm animals were sold. My son saw cows, calves, steers, pigs and sheep there.

No one wanted to take the children and me anywhere except to Church. My mother-in-law would come after us and take us to Church and bring us back. I knew how to drive and had my license, but Frank never let me use our car. My three children were my joy during this time.

Chapter 21 ~ *A Mix of Joy and Sorrow*

I did eventually go back to work. I hired a baby-sitter to care for Doris. When Doris started first grade, I was lonely and by choice, I became pregnant.

When the time to have the baby was close, my husband knew a week early that I would ENTER THE HOSPITAL. He planned to play cards that day and would not change his mind. A lady I knew lived nearby; she had a doctor's appointment that day. She came by to get me; I took my suitcase and entered the hospital alone.

Several days after the baby was born, Frank had not come to visit. I had to name the baby and I chose names I liked. I named her Kelly Lynn. When she was six weeks old I enrolled her in the Church as I had done for Wayne and Doris.

When we came home, I was thankful that Wayne watched everyone closely who touched Kelly Lynn. He wanted to make sure they cared for her just right.

I was not surprised when Frank began to keep me awake all night. He did not let my son sleep. Wayne would beg to go to bed, but Frank would put a chair in the middle of the room, and make him sit there all night. Frank would make him go to school the next day. This hurt me greatly because Wayne was so young. Frank didn't treat Doris badly; he merely ignored her.

When Kelly Lynn was old enough to walk, Frank would make her stand in a corner at night. She would get so tired she would cry. He would not let me put her to bed. Finally she would slump to the floor and fall asleep. I simply could not stand by and watch my children being harmed. The dynamics of having two young children, and a baby, a job and an abusive husband began to wear on me. The result was a COMPLETE BREAKDOWN from exhaustion. I ended up in the hospital for two weeks. I was supposed to rest, but I knew there would be no change when I returned home.

By this time we had moved to a house with more room. I decided to begin working the night shift. I was working at a pharmaceutical company. I realized that if I wasn't home AT NIGHT Frank had no reason to abuse my children. When I came home a neighbor came to care for Kelly Lynn, and I could sleep.

Our lives are better now, I thought. I was wrong. The life we had was headed for the worst time yet.

Chapter 22 ~ *Surprising Events*

Life began to change one day when I heard a knock on our door. Standing there was a person who had never come to my door before. This was my brother. He had come to inform me that my husband had called my mother. He was having me committed to a mental institution and would take away my children. Nothing could have surprised me about his ability to hurt me, but he had never expressed any interest in tending his children. This news astounded me. My brother stayed a few hours, trying to convince me to return with him. I refused because I was still in denial about my ability to be the perfect wife who could change my husband and save our marriage.

The next week, evidently because of another call from Frank, my sister showed up at my door. Her message was, "Leave now!" She and her husband worried for my safety. Their worry probably saved my life.

While everyone was asleep that night, my sister and her husband who had stayed, heard a noise; so he checked the room where I slept, and found my husband with his hands around my neck, trying to choke me. The next day I knew Frank's attempt to kill me, after various attempts had failed, meant that we had to leave. I called my mother and asked her to wire money so we could ride the bus to the city where she lived in Virginia.

I began to pack, and Frank's family came to the house to stop us. By now it was two o'clock in the morning. I had called the police to take us to the bus station.

I had to take my children from their beds and put them in the police car.

I was leaving behind the only life I knew. I prayed now begging God to guide me. This time I had three children to care for and be responsible for them. Could I do this alone? Of course not. I could RELY ON GOD to help me. He had kept me alive.

Chapter 23 ~ *Decisions to Make*

I was twenty-five years old. I had never lived on my own. We arrived in the city that seemed to be a concrete world.

My children and I hated such a world. We were met by my mother and stepfather; they took us to their home as we had no place to live.

The first thing I had to do was enroll my two older children in a school. The year was almost over, and if they didn't finish, they would have to repeat the grade.

My children had no clothes, shoes or toothbrushes. The next day my stepfather took me to the bank to find out if I had any funds, and if so, how much. I was clueless about our financial situation and had never even written a check. Drawing what money I could from the account, I purchased school clothes and supplies for my two children. My baby had to have clothes, but she didn't need much nor were my needs great.

My present job, which I had not left, opened the door for me to get a job in Pharmaceutical Research as a lab technician. The day I filled out my application I was hired before I had finished. Because this was April, and the financial year started in June, this qualified me for a week's vacation with pay.

This unexpected time allowed me to return and get things I had walked away from. With the two older children in school, I took my baby and caught the bus to go back. A friend met me and took the time to help me go to several places so I could get the children's school records and all the medical records. I closed any accounts with my name on them.

I quit the job where I had worked. By now my husband had found out about the bank accounts being empty. I knew I should leave quickly. I was almost finished when word reached me that my stepfather HAD A HEART ATTACK AND HAD DIED. He was the one who actually helped me to start a new life. Suddenly there was no one like him and I was devastated..

Chapter 24 ~ *Grieving*

Before I left to complete what I had not had time to do, I had found an apartment and was planning to move there. My step father had done everything to help me out of love, not from obligation. I felt he had been genuinely concerned for my welfare and for my children.

Immediately I had returned home. When I entered the house, I went straight to my mother to let her know I was very sorry for her loss. She turned away from me. Later I was blamed by my sister, saying, "This is all your fault. If you had not come here, and if my stepfather had not been under stress trying to help you, this would not have happened."

My stepsister disagreed since she knew her father had suffered previous heart attacks. In a fog, I dressed to go to the funeral home to help make the arrangements.

The funeral was a horrible experience of loss, regret, guilt, and despair. While in my heart I knew I wasn't responsible for my stepfather's death, yet knowing relatives around me blamed and resented my presence, my grief was deeper. All the steps my stepfather had taken to start me on a new life were cancelled.

After her husband's death, my mother collapsed and was hospitalized for some weeks. I tended to my mother's needs when she came home, so I stayed in her house. I took responsibility for her and her house since no one stepped forward for that. I also kept working so a babysitter took care of my children.

My sister did, however, take me to a lawyer who filed my divorce papers under constructive desertion: meaning my husband had deserted the marriage through his untenable treatment of me and the children.

I felt the need to start my children to live in our own home. I tried to be a good daughter to my mother, but there was a wall between us she would not bridge. Our conversations were awkward and not like the lively talks with my brothers and sister.

Chapter 25 ~ *My Family*

Finding an apartment was the next step. Since my childhood had been anything but normal, of great importance to me was the security of a safe home for my three children with a sense of peace and structure. They had already felt so much stress and upheavals, abuse and disorganization. They had been shifted here and there and had changed schools. Their possessions had been left behind. Surely they sensed the same disconnection from the family that I felt.

We had no furniture until my salary let me buy what I could. I had also brought back some of our things, and a few clothes in a small truck when we went back to the house one time. I was receiving no child support and my husband had filed for bankruptcy. We made it even though it was hard.

Every Friday we would walk to a small grocery store close by. I would buy several boxes of macaroni and two pounds of margarine. We had to be careful because my son and I took turns carrying the bags and the baby home. They ate that every night for dinner for two years and never complained. I would buy cereal and milk for breakfast. I supplemented with vitamins when I could.

When I came home from work, I spent all my time with my children until they were ready for bed. They seemed to know I was doing my best for them. They never got into any trouble at school. Each night I went to each of them and we talked about the day. Each one had this time with me. I wanted to make sure they did not go to bed hungry or needed to talk about any upsets. We always ended with bedtime prayers. It was a commitment I formed with them.

As time went by, I was able to save enough to buy a car. It was a straight shift: the kind I had learned to drive. I had all the amenities removed for a lower cost. (There's

God again providing for our needs). As the years passed I would let my son sit behind the steering wheel. That helped his self-esteem to pretend he was driving. My son loved the car; he kept it shining all the time. I made sure that each of my children learned to drive the car, so in the future they would be able to drive any car.

We never could take vacations, but we did some things for fun; many times we discovered these ourselves on weekends.

My children's father still caused trouble for us. On one occasion he pushed the apartment door open, slashed the furniture, and yanked the phone from the wall. The hard thing for me was that the children loved their grandparents. I didn't want to separate them from the children. Yet I was afraid for them to visit them. My husband had a brother who had a baby girl. His brother took her away, and she was never found, but he kept in touch with his mother. I was afraid that if I let my children visit them, one of them might disappear. I decided I would let them visit under supervision. After they were older I let them visit for a week. I trusted their grandfather, and told him they could only stay if he took responsibility for their safety. He always did as I asked so they saw the children frequently.

For years I tried to be an example by following a straight path. I certainly wasn't perfect and at times I had to hold back my feelings, when I had thoughts of getting back at Frank. I thought the one year of separation to make the divorce legal would never be over. When it was over he still persisted in making my life difficult.

Chapter 26 ~ *My Son Receives Attention; Trouble Again*

The children were growing; our finances were managed. I received raises at work; whoever needed new shoes or a coat was the one who benefited. I never took any time for myself and did not date anyone. I just wasn't interested. Only two years had passed since my divorce. I was still young and struggling to understand each new set of difficulties. I had more responsibilities than I had ever dreamed of having.

I worried that my son was not having any strong male influence. There were many young couples where we now lived. The young men soon took him under their wing. They took him to baseball games and when they ate out he was invited. They played football in the grass at the complex where we lived. It was such a relief to have others provide for him things he had never experienced and which I could not give him.

Once again Frank tried to cause misery. The stress was beyond endurance. He accused me of child neglect and told the police to lock me up. His accusations could not be proved. This was still a disturbance for me and the children. When the neighbors noticed police at our apartment, they immediately came to see if we needed help. They explained to the police that they helped my son play football with them. The Court had set up an injunction against Frank; he wasn't supposed to be anywhere around the city. The police warned him not to return.

During all this time I still saw things happening that let me know that I was not in charge. Frank paid someone to watch me. God was watching, too. These neighbors, for example: they didn't have to check about us, but they came.

Chapter 27 ~ *Surprising Changes*

One weekend the children were with their grandparents. I was alone when someone knocked on my door. Standing there was a man I knew from work. I was very surprised. He asked if I would go to the beach with him for the weekend.

"What makes you think I would go anywhere with you for two days?" I asked him. After talking with him and learning we would not be alone since his mother would be there, I thought, I have nothing to do, and no cash, why not get away for once? I accepted his invitation. I always kept in close touch with my mother by phone, so I phoned to let her know where I was going.

As soon as we were there, it was evident he was looking to start a relationship. Thank goodness his mother was there. I soon put an end to his idea.

But at work before the end of the next week, there were

some wild rumors which I made him retract right away. While we did not get off to a good start, I did go out with him, but never alone. He had two children. One was a girl the exact age as my YOUNGER DAUGHTER. He had visitation rights every other week. When he had his children, we would take them and mine out to eat. We also took some day trips together. He then met my mother who liked him right away. His mother met my mother and they were both amiable persons. After a while he asked me to marry him. I said, "No". I wanted to watch him and decide if he would be a good stepfather for my children. I would have to accept his children as my own.

After he asked me four more times, I entered into an agreement with him. In addition to becoming his wife, we would put our finances together and build a house where our children would attend good schools. They could bring friends home to spend the night if they wanted. I would take care of his children and treat them as my own. It wasn't a normal marriage but for the children it would be good.

Chapter 28 ~ *Working Three Jobs*

He did not turn out to be a good stepfather or even a good father. I had so carefully tried to make sure it was good. It wasn't until after we were married for a time, that I was told the money I made on my job was to be used for the family, and not to take care of the needs of my children. As a result I worked two jobs and later a third job. Once

I returned from my first job, I would fix dinner, and then take my children with me to my second job. While I worked, they did their homework. We always left at 9:00 so we would get home in time for baths and bed so they weren't tired during school the next day.

When they no longer wanted to go with me to work, and the two older children were approaching their teens, I went to a class to learn cake decorating and catering. I needed to bake birthday cakes for everyone and knowing how was less expensive than buying them. My schedule was a nightmare. I was always tired. My girls needed braces on their teeth and my son needed special eyeglasses. It seemed like they grew overnight so clothes and shoes were always an issue. For six years I had one day off from work to take the girls to orthodontists. Six thousand dollars later my girls had beautiful teeth.

I had no idea my cake decorating business would become full time. I made the first wedding cake at a friend's request; after that the requests were frequent. I had to narrow cake-making just to wedding cakes, and cater only holidays.

Chapter 29 ~ *Children, Friends and My Cake Business*

I was too busy, but it accomplished what I meant to do. I was at home with my children at night. I knew where they were, who their friends were, and most of their parents.

My children had a curfew which it seemed their friends did not have. My children were always together, and they had to be home earliest. Their friends weren't ready to break up, so they came to my home. They ordered pizza, watched movies, played cards, but I knew my children were home. I didn't go down and check on them, but I was awake until the last friend was gone. I did not allow alcohol or smoking.

Occasionally one friend would be having trouble at home and wanted to stay at my home. I thought a few days of separation would help mend things when they went home. They always had to call and get permission to stay, and to let their parents know where they were. I did not ask questions about the problem.

When I came home from work, prepared dinner, and cleaned up from that, I started making and baking cakes for the assembling of wedding cakes. I developed my own recipe for pound cakes because they were too expensive to make and then lose one. My recipe was ninety-nine per cent perfect. Of course the bride always had friends there who would also be brides before long. When they learned how I did the baking, they gave me most of their business. I never made two alike. I asked the bride to come to my house and view the special pans and actually plan her own cake. After she had decided the flowers she wanted, I could start making decorative flowers from the colored icing that I made. The mother of the bride had to approve of the cake when it was delivered for the reception, and pay in full. (I never had a complaint).

I loved this work, but sometimes I would decorate a cake until three A.M. and needed to be at my early job before seven A.M. Most of the weddings were Friday or Saturday night, so I would decorate the night before. I taught both of my girls how to decorate cakes. They soon had their own business of selling birthday cakes to their friends and their families. However, they wanted me to bake the cakes and make the icing. They had the fun of the decorating. They didn't know, but for me this was another way to be together. Then my son wanted to learn to cook and he became very good at that.

Chapter 30 ~ *College, Marriages, and Farewells*

The years passed and the time came for graduation for my son, next for the older daughter, and then my younger daughter, and my adopted daughter. My adopted son did not finish high school . He and his sister moved to another town. They kept in touch with me.

I wanted my children to have some higher education. I agreed to pay for them if their grades were good. This gave them strong motivation, and they had no loans to repay when they finished. Each one found a good job.

Weddings followed which I catered and directed to keep expenses low. My older daughter's wedding was two days before Christmas so the church and the cake decorations were red and white poinsettias. There was another wedding the same night, so I was really busy.

While my home life had lacked a caring relationship, I always knew I was loved through my children. After my younger daughter graduated, her wedding was in the spring, in May. Her cake and the reception table had spring flowers of purple, lavender, and pink with ivy leaves.

In a hurry one day I had a simple slip which was the beginning of a lengthy battle with pain. I fell on my right foot in such a way that the bones shattered in eight places. Surgery put the bones back together. My leg and foot were in a cast for two years. My foot never fully healed. For seven years the doctors could not understand my excruciating pain. They finally decided I had Chronic Regional Pain Syndrome. The RPS caused spinal problems. More surgery was done.

Unfortunately, the doctor who had operated on me before, ordered a medicine I was allergic to. My ARM BRACELET listed the medicines I was allergic to. Even though the nurse noticed the error, it could not be changed without the doctor's order. By the time he returned , I was in a coma. He had the tubes disconnected. When I was conscious, he had me dismissed in a few hours.

Later, when I tried to get my file from him, he was gone. I will stop with these memories.

My mother was diagnosed with cancer during this time. She did not want treatment. I prepared meals for her and took them to her. Sometimes my health prevented driving, and other plans were needed. My sister and her husband visited our mother in the evenings. I phoned her when I could not get there. The day came when the doctor informed us her death would occur soon. My siblings and I went to her hospital room. I sat by her side until she passed from this life.

Chapter 31 ~ My Co-Workers and Retiring

My workplace environment gave me a great deal of joy. In my work as a lab technician, I worked with people from many countries. All of my co-workers were close. I loved my work and socialized a little. We began having dinners at each home with ethnic food at each one. This was new to me: to enjoy the dinners with my friends.

I had worked hard so many years, that it had taken a toll on my body. My health was compromised, and it wasn't long before several doctors decided I would have to retire on disability. It was the end of twenty-five years of good times and trying times. At least I had each of my children settled. It was what I had asked God for many years before, "Please let me have good health long enough to raise my children." My request was granted and I was so grateful.

Chapter 32 ~ New Problems

I am not sure why or how I continually ended up with people intent on humiliating me and abusing me psychologically, but in this marriage the problem was finances. You wouldn't think I would still be quiet and shy, but I always hated trouble.

Now my husband's lying was so great that I DECIDED HE DIDN'T KNOW TRUTH FROM FICTION. He had no concept of finances. When I tried to explain we did not have enough funds in our account to support all his wants, he would walk away. If he wanted a new truck, or a boat, or a piece of land he bought it. He never thought about how it would be paid for because that was my problem. I had worked so hard for many years that seeing my savings vanish to make my husband happy was not sensible.

It seemed like things became stressful beyond reason. At first I didn't notice some things especially when I completely trusted someone. My stress went out of control. My husband insisted that I see a psychiatrist so I did. That was not the answer. I REMEMBERED TO GO TO THE ONLY ONE I COULD FOR HELP: GOD. No answer. Things got worse when my mind wouldn't work. I finally admitted myself to a mental ward at a hospital. I knew I had to get away. That doctor saw patients there. Because I admitted myself, I could come and go as I wanted. I did not have to go to any sessions the doctors had.

The women there began to come to my room and talk to me. They would sit on my bed or on the floor and ask me questions. Their questions always had something about why they were there. They said they noticed I was different, and didn't belong there. So I talked to them and many of the answers to their questions were in the Holy

Bible. I would turn to where certain verses were and I would read what would help them. The clinicians did not approve that the women came to talk to me. I certainly had no training to help these women, but maybe I was supposed to help because I WAS THERE.

I did not learn until later that my husband had paid the psychiatrist to have me committed to a mental institution permanently. Then he could get a divorce quickly and everything we had would be his. This did not happen since I had admitted myself.

Chapter 33 ~ *New Chances*

My children knew some things they had not told me. One night my older daughter Doris said, "Mom, I want to take you for a ride." I told her I did not like to go out after dark. She insisted it would not take long. I agreed to go with her. There was a place on a main street where pickup trucks parked every Friday night. Couples with lawn chairs and coolers watched traffic going by and sometimes they yelled things at the drivers. As we approached we slowed down; there was my husband with a girl at least twenty-five years younger than me. Now, I finally understood why my husband was acting against me. I couldn't believe what I saw.

No doubt he had promised her our house and everything in it. He had to get me away first and not give me any money. The doctor was a part of his plan. I think it was meant for me to be at the hospital during the time I was there. After that night I had all the locks of the doors changed. I did not allow my husband to return. He had an apartment by now. Those sixteen years of my life with him were ended.

I had a new life now. I had finished paying for my younger daughter's college and wedding. I had planned to work for my retirement. Because of the doctors' advice about my health, I retired on disability.

"God doith as He willith," I learned later, and that had to be God's will. I wasn't a Baha'i yet, but when I learned more, I believed that everything that happened to me WAS ALLOWED TO LEAD ME IN A NEW DIRECTION.

Chapter 34 ~ *A Life Changing Decision*

My income was not large enough to take care of this large house. My Pastor continually told me I should sell it and move into an apartment I could afford. I wouldn't have to worry about the money I did not have. Finally, I took his advice and sold the house. It was not a happy day. I moved to what seemed was a small apartment. I met all my new neighbors and after a few weeks I felt better about having moved.

I had a neighbor who lived upstairs from me. Every time I saw her she had a smile. She was always pleasant. She never gossiped about anyone, and was always peaceful. She had something that I wanted. We became good friends; she did things to help me. When the time came I did something she needed. We would go for long rides and talk.

One day I asked her about her religion. She was hesitant to answer, but I persisted. She gave me some brochures about the Baha'i Faith. I read them over and over again, but I did not understand. I asked her questions; she said she would send someone to talk to me. A man came and told me some information, but I did not understand. He told me to write the questions I had and he would return the next week. I wrote and wrote; there was so much I wanted to know. My friend and I continued to spend more time together and I kept asking questions. She tried to give me answers, but decided to give me more pamphlets. She still was someone I wanted to be like. Her friend returned and I HAD ABOUT ONE HUNDRED QUESTIONS for him. He answered many of them. When he came again the next week, I had more questions. He just could not seem to answer them all. He invited me to a feast. He did not tell me what a feast was and I expected a lot of food. I met people who lived in my county and I learned they were called a community. (Coffee and cookies were served after prayer and readings.) For sixty years I had been a Baptist and was happy in that religion. I could not believe that I knew I needed to change so quickly. I decided one day that even though I did not know enough, that this new Faith was meant for me. I was ready to change. My journey began by learning a new language - a kind of music - in the writings of the Founder, Baha'u'llah. I didn't have to do anything but listen.

Many people from my Church tried to talk me out of changing. They even brought me information about the Baha'is that was negative. It didn't seem to matter to me. My son wanted to know just what I was getting myself into. I arranged a meeting with the men of the community and him. I didn't attend so he could ask anything he wanted. He told me afterwards that it seemed like a good thing to him, and he would not worry about me. My daughters could not understand why I changed my religion. They distanced themselves from me. My siblings felt the same way. I sent cards to each of my nine grandchildren who knew I had become a Baha'i. I included a small gift for each one explaining this was how I was observing the Baha'i New Year. I also gave them the website for the Baha'is so they could read information for themselves, www.bahai.us and www.bahai.org. After the meeting with my son, I did sign my card and I became a member of the Baha'i Faith.

My friend talked with me openly and I learned even more by talking with her. She corrected me when I mispronounced the Name of Baha'u' llah (the Founder). It seemed like all the members knew so much and I wanted to learn more. I read 28 books and pamphlets the first year. Later, as I read them over again, I realized I hadn't understood them because I read them too fast.

I began taking my turn to host a feast and devotions. By now my medical condition kept me home, except for doctor appointments. All the meetings were held at my home. Next, I learned about the Ruhi Book Study Circles, and I wanted to learn from them. All of those in the Study Circles agreed to study in my home. I studied the books: one through eight. This took many months. I qualified to be a tutor for other members and seekers wanting to study the books.

A new illness caused me to be in the hospital for six months. This included two episodes of pneumonia.

Anyone who came to help me or visit me became a seeker or showed interest in the Baha'i Faith; I would invite them to return. I would give them the internet address of the Baha'i Faith and many were curious enough to go to the site and do some reading. That was one way of passing along news of the new Faith I had embraced.

I had many neighbors at the apartments where I lived. When I had recovered I would have parties and invite them. I knew they came for the food, but it gave me a chance to introduce them to the Baha'i Faith and what we stood for. I talked to people every chance I had about my new Faith.

Chapter 35 ~ *My Baha'i Life*

This is more about my Baha'i life. I knew about the Bab (the Forerunner), and Baha'u'llah (the Founder or Manifestation), and 'Abdu'l Baha (His son), and Shoghi Effendi (the Guardian). Where was Jesus going to fit in? I knew that I understood and accepted how this new Faith began. I just didn't know what to do with some things I had believed for so long. In His writings Baha'u'llah referred to Jesus and quotes the Quran several times. His teachings update the teachings of the Messengers who came in the past centuries. The purpose of the Ruhi Books is to share the life of Baha'u'llah, and how to serve the community. I began to understand better.

I also learned what it meant to go on Pilgrimage to the places in Israel where Baha'u'llah had lived and to the Shrine where He is buried. I knew my health would prevent me from such travel. I enjoyed hearing other members tell about their trips and seeing photos they took.

As soon as I became a Baha'i, I became a member of the Local Spiritual Assembly. They needed one more member and I was the one. I learned so much more. They discussed business but personal affairs were not talked about. Decisions were made according to one's conscience. I had never decided anything about Church so this was different. I had been active in Churches, but making decisions was the role of a board. I had to have more knowledge so I could make right decisions in our assembly. I had read the Bible two times. It seemed that God guided people from the beginning of time (or Genesis) by His inspiration. I would rely on His guidance.

For special devotional meetings as part of my hosting, I would bake and decorate several cakes with the nine-pointed Baha'i star symbol. When our meeting was over most of the people took pieces of cake with them to share with their families.

As a professional cake decorator and caterer, I reserved the space in the community room to prepare for a Baha'i wedding. This was a distinct honor for our community. Our Baha'i lady had met a Baha'i man from Scotland when they were in England. Both were going on pilgrimage to Baha'i Holy Shrines. They became friends instantly. They kept in close contact and learned about each other over Skype for more than a year. They became engaged over Skype!

He came to the United States to visit and to decide if he would like to live here. He stayed for several weeks. Some Baha'is took him on day trips. Many of us met him when he was visiting, and we loved and accepted him.

He returned to England to arrange his affairs so he could become a citizen of the United States. The wedding was planned for the day after he arrived back. The community room was transformed into a garden. The bride's friends had brought a great variety of fresh flowers.

A member of our community officiated the couple's wedding vows. A beautiful reception was held afterwards. They were now both members of our community. As partners they blessed our community greatly.

A few years later I heard someone mention about a new prayer group. I asked about it. I learned that James

Williams was starting a Prayer Circle five days a week on Skype. It would begin at nine A.M. Eastern time and last forty-five minutes. I phoned him to be on the list to be called. The list grew quickly; most of the original members are still called. Others have joined through the years. We have prayers, chants, beautiful songs, and sometimes Baha'i news at the end. Members come from many states: the East coast, the South, the West, and the Congo at times. It is rare for me to miss a day. It makes the day begin right.

Chapter 36 ~ *Healing Happens For My Eyes*

For part of my life, I couldn't see well enough to read! I was told I would lose my eyesight. A lady from Michigan took the time to print some prayers in large print so I could participate better. I had been listening and had not been reading. Having worked in Pharmaceutical research, I refused to accept the doctor's diagnosis. I thought of a "formula" to stop my sight from becoming worse than it was. (The doctors did not know the cause of the problem and I had surgery twice.) I decided to give myself two hours a day to use my eyes. This would include reading my mail and praying my Baha'i Prayers. When the two hours were used, I stopped reading. I did this for three months. Then I went back to be tested. I had to know if my formula was helping me. It had to be an unbiased test. My eyesight tested PERFECT! The doctors were amazed! I told no one what I was doing. I knew I would have to continue this schedule the rest of my life or my eyes could get worse. Each day I decide what is most important to read.

I am thankful to have a tape player for hearing books from a library. I should mention that my sight allows me to drive to doctor appointments. If I have fallen, I call 9-1-1. Health care workers have helped me in my home. What I want to do is use opportunities to share my faith. I pray to change my heart completely; to have hope in the gift of knowledge and understanding is my desire. I am so thankful. I am so much more aware as a Baha'i. I wonder what Baha'u'llah has for me in the future!!! I am thankful also for each of Baha'u'llah's servants who help me every day in some way.

Chapter 37 ~ *My Special Dog, Princess*

I worked for the pharmaceutical company for 25 years doing research to benefit dogs. I tested formulas for new drugs. I assisted in surgeries. I held strange dogs in my arms as they were put to sleep. It is important that you know this so you know that these events are true and were not caused by panic, or what I didn't know. I knew too much. You know I had several kinds of illnesses after I retired. I learned that service dogs are available for people with various handicaps. I had several Pekinese dogs over the years for service.

This story is about Princess, my companion dog. This was the night of Monday, January 23, 2012. I had taken Princess that day to her veterinarian, Dr. Z. She was to go to a special group at an animal hospital on Wednesday hoping to find some help. Dr. Z. gave her some fluids to help her until Wednesday. That night I was holding Princess in my arms; she was limp and her breathing was slowing. I called Dr. Z. for advice. I didn't know the office was closed, but all the employees were gathered in the waiting room. As the doctor began talking to me, the phone was on speaker.

The girls all knew Princess and me and were listening. Dr. Z. told me that Princess was dying and to hold her in my arms. "I am doing that," I said.

I hung the phone up. I cried my heart out as I held her. I wasn't ready to let her go after having her sixteen years. I prayed to God to let me have a little more time with her. No one knows how God counts time; I hoped she could still be alive in the morning. I stayed awake and watched her. At midnight, she came to the foot of her crib to let me know she wanted something. (This has always been her way of waking me up when she needed something.) At this moment I knew my prayer had been answered. I put her back in her crib. She wasn't finished yet. I took her to her water bowl, and she drank. Again in her crib she looked at me. I was sure she couldn't eat food. But I fixed her some baby food and took it to my bedroom. I put the bowl on my sheets, where I had thrown the covers back. I picked her up, and put her by the bowl of food. I put my arm around her because I thought she was weak. She ate the food. She and I did this three times until she had eaten what had been in the jar. Truly, she was "my miracle girl!" I hugged her happily, thanking God. I laid her in her crib. She lay down and slept all night. On Tuesday morning she was standing on four strong legs, waiting for me to put her on the floor. I watched as she walked slowly down the hall. I took her outside to the grass a few minutes.

I took her to be seen by Dr. Z. She walked on her own through the door to the waiting room. Everyone who had heard my conversation the night before came to see her. They found it hard to believe she was walking.

I took her to a hospital for service and companion dogs only. X-rays showed she had arthritis, but they could not help that. By Friday she was eating her regular food. Many people shared in the miracle that day. I kept Princess for eight more months. Then I was ready to let her leave me. I know God doesn't always answer prayers the way we want but HE DOES ANSWER them.

Some Favorite Baha'i Prayers

For Children
O God, guide me, protect me, make of me a shining lamp and a brilliant star. Thou are the Mighty and the Powerful.
> *~ 'Abdu'l- Baha*

For Everyone
O Thou Whose tests are a healing medicine to such as are nigh unto Thee, Whose sword is the ardent desire of all them that love Thee, Whose dart is the dearest wish of those hearts that yearn after Thee, Whose decree is the sole hope of them that have recognized Thy truth! I implore Thee, by Thy divine sweetness and by the splendors of the glory of Thy face, to send down upon us from Thy retreats on high that which will enable us to draw nigh unto Thee. Set, then, our feet firm, O my God, in Thy Cause, and enlighten our hearts with the effulgence of Thy knowledge, and illumine our breasts with the brightness of Thy names.
> *~ Bahá'u'lláh*

The purpose for writing this book, is for anyone who would be in a life threatening situation and you want to leave it, you must know before you attempt to leave, that your life will be difficult. You must prepare yourself. In this age, you may look for advice from many sources. It is possible with God's help for a better life for you. To God be the glory and thanks.

Thanks go to Meg Wegs who has edited this edition of my autobiography.
Thank you, Meg

Made in the USA
Middletown, DE
17 August 2016